Book 1:
Cooking for One
Cookbook for Beginners

By Claire Daniels

&

Book 2:
Slow Cooking Guide for
Beginners

By Claire Daniels

&

Book 3:
Wok Cookbook for Beginners

By Claire Daniels

Book 1:

Cooking for One

Cookbook for Beginners

By Claire Daniels

The Ultimate Recipe Cookbook for Cooking for One!

Cooking Books Box Set #17: Cooking for One Cookbook for Beginners & Slow
Cooking Guide for Beginners & Wok Cookbook for Beginners

Table Of Contents

Introduction

I want to thank you and congratulate you for purchasing the book, *"Cooking for One Cookbook for Beginners: The Ultimate Recipe Cookbook for Cooking for One!"*

This book contains proven steps and strategies on how to prepare fast, easy and delicious one serving meals.

If you are a bachelor or a bachelorette and if you are living in an apartment or in a dormitory, then this book is written especially for you! Everyone deserves to enjoy a home cooked meal, and you don't have to overspend or risk spoilage to have that every day. Here you will find tips and plenty of recipes to keep your taste buds and healthy fully satisfied. So say goodbye to takeouts and TV dinners because you are about to give your mealtime a major makeover.

Thanks again for purchasing this book, I hope you enjoy it!

Chapter 1 - Important "Cooking for One" Tips

You got this book for a reason: you are tired of microwave TV dinners, canned food and unhealthy takeouts. You want to enjoy fast, delicious, cheap and healthy meals that will make eating alone a worthwhile experience. Well, good news, for this book will guide you through the journey of healthier eating!

From now on, your kitchen will be your best friend. If there is something about your kitchen that you don't like (such as the paint on the walls) then go ahead and change it. You will be spending a bit more time in this part of your home so why not make it a fun experience every time.

One big advantage of cooking for one is that dish washing won't be such a chore. All you will ever need is one pair of cutlery, one bowl, one plate, one cup and one glass. And just because you're cooking for one does not make it a rush all of the time. Dedicate a table and a chair to be your dining area, spread an attractive tablecloth over it and place a vase with some fresh cut flowers in it. Create a playlist to serve as your background music while you are eating to set the right ambiance. Hang a lantern over a light bulb to set the mood for eating at home.

The dining experience aside, you will want to have the sharpest equipment at hand in your kitchen in order to prepare your meals.

What You'll Need in a Kitchen for One
You won't be required to purchase kitchen equipment suitable for a chef. In fact, this book is especially written with people from small apartments and dormitories in mind. Let's go by the principle of working with what you have; only buy additional kitchen equipment if you have set aside a specific budget for it.

Here is a list of necessary items in your kitchen, enumerated based on importance:

- **A sharp knife.** If there is one necessary tool in your kitchen, then it should be this. You will need it in most recipes, from slicing meat to chopping vegetables.

- **Two bowls, a large one and a small one.** The smaller bowl is where you will be eating most of your meals from, while the larger bowl will make salad tossing an easier affair.

- **A nonstick frying pan and spatula.** Using nonstick will make it a breeze to wash and will spare you from using oil while cooking.

- **Hot plate.** This will make cooking for one a lot cheaper compared to using a stove top. That's because it can be used anywhere no matter how small your living space may be.

- **A small rice cooker.** This nifty little appliance will stretch beyond plain old rice and let you cook a wide array of dishes.

- **A toaster oven.** It is far more practical to use this for broiling and baking because it does not take long to heat up.

- **A personal refrigerator.** This is the last on the list because it is quite a luxury. However, if you can afford it then it truly is a worthwhile investment.

Fridge-free Cooking

In case you don't have a refrigerator yet, you will not be able to stockpile on any ingredients that would require it. Thankfully, many grocery stores offer individual or travel-sized servings. Even if they are not as cheap as bulk, you will still end up saving more money compared to them getting spoiled. Locate the nearest grocery store that offers individual servings in your daily route or near your home.

In the meantime, you can keep your food items in a cooler that is packed with ice. Just ensure that you've got the food sealed tightly in containers since the ice will still continue to melt.

Plan your Meals Ahead

The secret to successfully staying within your budget and enjoying delicious one serving meals at the same time is through planning. Set aside an hour each week and dedicate it to planning your breakfast, lunch and dinner meals.

A meal plan will serve as your guide for purchasing the right ingredients since you will know exactly what to do with them once you get home. Even eating out and takeouts can be included in your plan, especially during days when you simply do not have energy left to prepare a dish yourself.

Also, you can cook in bulk and divide the servings into separate containers which you can simply grab and heat up during mealtimes. This method will certainly save you a lot of money and time in the long run.

Chapter 2 - Fast and Easy Breakfast Recipes

Singles are usually out and about, which means preparing breakfast at home should beat purchasing expensive coffee and waffles from a cafe. Here are 6 fast and easy breakfast recipes that you can whip up within 5 to 20 minutes. Pair any one of these meals with a cup of hot coffee or a glass of orange juice.

Rice Cereal

Prep Time: 10 to 15 minutes.

Ingredients:

- 1 cup cooked rice (leftover rice is fine, just heat it up if you put it in the fridge)
- 1/4 cup milk (dairy or nut-based)
- 1 Tbsp. of finely chopped nuts (almonds, pecans, hazelnuts, etc)
- A piece of fresh or dried fruit (the ones in season are the cheapest)
- A generous dash of allspice, nutmeg and/or cinnamon
- Salt (a small pinch)
- Honey, agave or maple syrup (as much as you like)

Instructions:

1. In a nonstick pan, mash up your rice with your fork until it becomes mushy.

2. Pour in the milk and place over low heat for about 5 to 10 minutes. In the meantime, chop up your piece of fruit and then add that to the mixture.

3. Lightly toast the chopped nuts.

4. Remove the rice cereal from the pan and into your bowl. Sprinkle the nuts on top and then drizzle your honey, agave or maple syrup on top. Enjoy!

An American Breakfast

Prep Time: 10 to 15 minutes

Ingredients:

- 1 strip of fresh bacon (unseasoned and unprocessed)

- 1 egg
- 1 or 2 slices of whole grain bread
- Optional: a sliver of margarine or butter (for your toast)
- Salt and Pepper

Instructions:

1. Heat up your nonstick pan over low-medium.

2. Cut your bacon into bite-sized pieces. Season with salt and pepper.

3. Place them on the pan and turn the heat up to medium. Let each side cook for 5 minutes.

4. Pop your bread into your toaster for 2 minutes.

5. Two minutes after turning the pieces of bacon, move them to the side and crack your egg open in the same pan.

6. Season your egg with a bit of salt and pepper. Tip the pan a bit to let its runny whites pour to its edges and become cooked.

7. Remove the egg and bacon from pan and transfer onto plate. Place toast on the side. Enjoy!

French Toast

Prep Time: 5 to 10 minutes

Ingredients:

- 2 or 3 slices of bread
- 1 egg
- 1/4 cup of milk (dairy or nut-based)
- 1 tsp of butter or oil
- Vanilla
- Salt
- Jam, butter, syrup or applesauce

Instructions:

1. In a small bowl, crack the egg and add salt and vanilla. Beat until foamy.

2. Soak the slices of bread in the egg mixture for as long as you can.

3. Heat a nonstick pan over medium and melt the butter or drizzle the oil on top.

4. Place the soaked bread in the pan and cook well. Flip once the underside is golden brown.

5. Once both sides are golden brown, remove from pan and serve on plate with a side of jam, butter, syrup or applesauce. Enjoy!

Breakfast Burrito

Prep Time: 5 to 10 minutes

Ingredients:

- 1 or 2 eggs
- 1 tortilla or pita
- 1/4 cup chopped spinach or any other greens of choice
- 2 or 3 slices of any type of cheese
- Salt and pepper
- Optional: 1 fresh tomato (diced) and salsa

Instructions:

1. Place a nonstick pan over low-medium heat and heat up the greens and diced tomato. Add a dash of salt and pepper.

2. Set veggies aside and cook the egg on the same pan (you can choose to do scrambled or sunny side up).

3. Place the cheese on top of the egg to melt it a bit.

4. Put all of the ingredients inside your tortilla or pita. Add salsa if desired. Enjoy!

Ham and Cheese Omelet

Prep Time: 5 to 10 minutes

Ingredients:

- 1 slice of ham (from the deli)
- 1 to 2 eggs
- Handful of cheese (Feta, Parmesan, Prosciutto, etc)
- Salt and pepper
- Optional: 1 small onion, sliced thinly
- Drizzle of oil (preferably olive or coconut)

Instructions:

1. Dice the ham.

2. Beat the eggs in a shallow bowl and add a dash of salt and pepper before beating it again until foamy.

3. Heat up a nonstick pan over low-medium. Once it starts to get hot, add some oil.

4. Heat up your diced ham. Transfer to a plate and set aside.

5. Sautee your sliced onion. Gradually pour in the beaten eggs. Keep adding until the underside is almost completely cooked.

6. Tilt the pan slightly to allow the runny egg mixture to fall directly on the surface of the pan and become cooked.

7. Place your ham at the center, followed by the cheese. Carefully fold the omelet. If it gets messed up, it's alright for it will still be delicious.

8. Transfer the omelet to a plate and cut across the center to let steam out. Enjoy!

Instant Muesli

Prep Time: 3 minutes

Ingredients:

- 1/4 cup nuts and seeds (a mixture of your favorites, such as walnuts, sunflower seeds, almonds, etc.)

- 1/2 cup rolled oats

- A piece of fresh or dried fruit

- Milk (dairy or nut-based)

- Optional: honey and 1 Tbsp of ground flax seeds

Instructions:

1. Slice up the fruit.

2. Combine all of the dry ingredients in your bowl.

3. Pour in the milk and let the ingredients soak it up to soften. Enjoy!

Chapter 3 - Lunchbox-Ready Lunch Recipes

Lunchtime is usually crunch time, especially for busy singles. However, that is no excuse to always grab an unhealthy lunch that will cause a wide range of illnesses in the long run. Instead, treat yourself to these 5 healthy and delicious lunch recipes that you can easily take with you to work or school.

If you have a lunch buddy who also cooks for one, you can talk to them about preparing lunches for each other. For instance, you will be the one to prepare lunch on Mondays, him/her on Tuesdays, and so on. This is a great way to save on prep time and your budget. Simply double the measurements in the ingredients to make two servings.

Cuban Sandwich

Prep Time: 3 to 5 minutes

Ingredients:

- 2 slices of whole wheat bread
- 4 to 6 slices of baked ham
- 2 slices of cheese of your choice
- 2 slices of dill pickle
- 1/2 tsp butter
- mustard

Instructions:

1. On a plate, lay the two slices of bread and spread a thin layer of mustard on one side of each.

2. Place one slice of each ingredient on top of each slice of bread, beginning with the ham, followed by the cheese and finally the pickle slices.

3. Sandwich the two sets of layers together.

4. Butter the outer part of the sandwich.

5. Heat a nonstick frying pan over medium. Place the sandwich in and press it down using a spatula for 1 to 2 minutes. Flip and repeat.

6. Remove from the pan once the sandwich is golden brown and the cheese has melted. Eat immediately or wrap in tin foil as packed lunch.

Good-for-one Tuna Spaghetti

Prep Time: 20 minutes

Ingredients:

- 1 fistful of spaghetti pasta
- 1/2 cup marinara sauce
- 2 Tbsp. parmesan cheese
- 1 small can of tuna (in brine or oil)
- 1 small red onion, sliced thinly
- 2 cloves garlic, crushed and diced
- Salt and paper
- Optional: brown sugar
- Olive oil

Instructions:

1. Heat a small pot full of water on the stove or hot plate. Add a dash of salt and a drizzle of oil. Let it boil.

2. Once it starts to boil, place your pasta into the water; it's alright if half of the strands are not submerged because they will eventually once the lower half starts to soften. Follow the manufacturer's instructions on how long the pasta should be boiled.

3. Remove pasta when al dente and drain. Set aside.

4. Drain the tuna.

5. Heat a nonstick pan on low-medium. Add a drizzle of olive oil. Sautee onion and garlic.

6. After the onions have become translucent, add the tuna and a dash of salt and pepper. Cook until tuna becomes a bit dry.

7. Add the marinara sauce and stir. Taste your sauce to check the flavor. You can add some brown sugar if you want to make it a bit sweet.

8. Remove the sauce once it is thoroughly heated and pour over your pasta. Add parmesan cheese on top. Eat immediately or pack in an airtight container for lunch on-the-go.

Broiled Tomato Sandwich

Prep Time: 10 minutes

Ingredients:

- 1 large or 2 small ripe tomatoes, sliced
- 1/2 Tbsp olive oil
- 1/2 Tbsp balsamic vinegar
- 1/2 Tbsp mayonnaise
- A pinch of dried parsley and dried oregano
- A pinch of black pepper
- 1/2 Tbsp Parmesan Cheese
- 2 slices of whole wheat bread

Instructions:

1. Lightly toast the two slices of bread.

2. Preheat toaster oven to broil.

3. Whisk olive oil and vinegar together in a small bow. Soak sliced tomatoes in marinade.

4. In another bowl, create a spread with the mayonnaise, black pepper, oregano, parsley and some of the Parmesan cheese. Spread over toast.

5. Put the marinated tomatoes on top of the toast with spread and sprinkle the rest of the Parmesan cheese on top.

6. Put the toast with the tomatoes on your toaster tray and broil for 3 to 5 minutes or until the cheese turns golden brown. You can sandwich the two slices together and wrap it in tin foil if you plan to pack it for lunch.

Bacon Mushroom Chicken

Cooking Books Box Set #17: Cooking for One Cookbook for Beginners & Slow Cooking Guide for Beginners & Wok Cookbook for Beginners

Prep Time: 1 hour and 5 minutes.

Ingredients:

- 1 boneless chicken breast
- 1 or 2 thick strips of bacon
- 1 Tbsp melted butter
- 1/2 tsp salt
- Dash of garlic powder
- 1/4 cup mushrooms, sliced into halves
- 3 Tbsp heavy cream

Instructions:

1. Preheat oven to 350 degrees F (or 175 degrees C).

2. Spread the melted butter into a small, deep baking dish that is big enough to fit your chicken breast. Place the chicken breast in the dish with the skin side facing downward.

3. Season chicken with salt and garlic powder. Turn and season the other side. Lay bacon strips over the chicken and top with mushrooms.

4. Bake in the oven for 45 to 60 minutes, or until the chicken juices come out clear.

5. Take the bacon mushroom chicken out onto a plate.

6. Collect the juices and pour into a small pan. Add heavy cream and whisk over low heat until you get a thick sauce. Pour over the chicken. Enjoy!

Classic BLT

Prep Time: 10 minutes

Ingredients:

- 2 slices of whole wheat bread
- 2 lettuce leaves
- 2 tomato slices

Cooking Books Box Set #17: Cooking for One Cookbook for Beginners & Slow Cooking Guide for Beginners & Wok Cookbook for Beginners

- 4 bacon strips

- 1 Tbsp mayonnaise

Instructions:

1. Place a nonstick pan over medium-high heat and cook bacon strips until brown. Drain the oil and places strips on paper towels.

2. Toast the bread slices.

3. Layer the bacon strips, lettuce and tomato slices on a slice of toast and spread mayonnaise on one side of the other toast. Sandwich slices together. Pack it up in tin foil to keep warm, otherwise eat immediately.

Chapter 4 - Classic and Delectable Dinner Recipes

Dinner should be a truly enjoyable experience, even if it is only yourself and your favorite music or TV show. Make dining at home an everyday luxury without overspending by cooking any one of these delectable recipes and pairing the dish with a glass of wine and a dinner roll or two. And if you really like the recipe then you can go ahead and double up the ingredients, then pack it up for reheating at lunchtime the next day.

Baked Salmon

Prep Time: 3 minutes preparation, 1 hour marination, and 45 minutes baking time

Ingredients:

- 1 clove garlic, minced

- 3 Tbsp olive oil

- 1/2 tsp dried basil

- 1/2 tsp salt

- 1/2 tsp ground black pepper

- 1/2 Tbsp lemon juice

- 1/2 Tbsp chopped fresh parsley

- 1 6-oz. Fillet salmon

Instructions:

1. Combine the lemon juice, salt and pepper, olive oil, garlic and parsley in a small bowl.

2. Place the fillet in a glass baking dish and pour the marinade on top.

3. Marinate in the refrigerator or cooler for 30 minutes, turn the fillet over, and then marinate for another 30 minutes.

4. Preheat oven to 375 degrees F (or 190 degrees C).

5. Put the salmon fillets in tin foil along with the marinade, then close the tin foil tightly. Put in a glass dish and into the oven.

6. Bake for 45 minutes or until fillet can easily be flaked.

Baked Falafel

Prep Time: 30 minutes

Ingredients:

- 1 egg
- 1 small onion, chopped
- Half a can of garbanzo beans (place the other half in an airtight container with the juices and refrigerate)
- 3 Tbsp chopped fresh parsley
- 1 clove garlic
- 1/2 tsp ground cumin
- A pinch of ground coriander, salt and baking soda
- 1/2 Tbsp all-purpose flour
- 1 tsp olive oil

Instructions:

1. Rinse and drain the garbanzo beans.

2. Beat the egg until foamy.

3. Place onion between two sheets of heavy duty kitchen towels and press hard to get rid of moisture. Set aside.

4. Using a food processor, coarsely puree garbanzo beans, parsley, garlic, coriander, salt and baking soda. Combine the mixture with the onion.

5. Add the beaten egg and flour into the mixture and form into two large balls. Flatten the balls on a plate and set aside for 15 minutes.

6. Preheat oven to 400 degrees F (or 200 degrees C).

7. Place an oven-safe frying pan over medium-high heat. Drizzle olive oil in pan and fry patties until golden brown on both sides.

8. Place the skillet into the oven and bake for 10 minutes. Enjoy!

Savory Garlic Steaks

(If possible, marinate steaks in fridge/cooler for 25 to 48 hours before cooking.)

Prep Time: 20 to 30 minutes.

Ingredients:

- 1 1/2-lb. rib-eye steak
- 1/4 cup balsamic vinegar
- 3 Tbsp soy sauce
- 1 1/2 Tbsp minced garlic
- 1 Tbsp honey
- 1 Tbsp olive oil
- 1 tsp black pepper
- 1/2 tsp Worcestershire sauce
- 1/2 tsp onion powder
- A pinch of salt
- A pinch of cayenne pepper
- Optional: 1/4 tsp liquid smoke flavoring

Instructions:

1. Combine the vinegar, soy sauce, Worcestershire sauce, honey, olive oil, garlic, black pepper, onion powder, salt, cayenne pepper and liquid smoke in a small bowl.

2. In a shallow dish, put the steak in and pour the marinade on top. Coat the entire steak and rub it into the meat. Cover the dish and allow to marinate in the fridge or cooler for 24 to 48 hours.

3. Place grill on medium-high heat.

4. Spray or brush some oil on the grill and grill the steak for 7 minutes for each side. Rub some of the marinade on the steak as you grill. Enjoy!

Recipe Stuffed Pork Chops with Apple and Gorgonzola

Prep Time: 1 hr and 30 minutes

Ingredients:

- 1 thick cut pork chop

- 1/4 cup chopped Granny Smith apples

- 2 Tbsp Gorgonzola cheese, crumbled

- 1/2 Tbsp butter

- 1 tsp dried thyme

- 1 clove garlic, minced

- A drizzle of olive oil

- 1 1/2 Tbsp dry sherry

- 1 Tbsp heavy cream

- 3 Tbsp chicken broth

- Salt and black pepper

Instructions:

1. Preheat the oven to 375 degrees F (or 190 degrees C).

2. Prepare the apple stuffing: put a frying pan on medium heat, put the butter in and saute the chopped apples, thyme and add a pinch of salt and pepper for 15 minutes or until apple softens.

3. Put mixture in a bowl and add 1 tablespoon of Gorgonzola cheese. Mix well.

4. Cut the pork chop across from the fat to the bone to make a butterfly cut. Stuff the center with the apple mixture. Set aside 1 or 2 tablespoons of the mixture.

5. Bake the pork chop for 60 minutes.

6. Remove pork chop from the oven and place on a plate. Add the remaining apple mixture around the chop.

7. Place a nonstick pan over low heat and saute the garlic. Add the cheese and allow to melt. Add sherry, cream, half of the chicken stock, and a pinch of salt and pepper. Mix well.

8. Stir until sauce starts to thicken. Add the rest of the chicken stock and stir. Drizzle the sauce over the pork chop.

Pita Chicken

Prep Time: 15 minutes

Ingredients:

- 1 skinless and boneless chicken breast
- 1/2 Tbsp olive oil
- A dash of garlic powder and onion powder
- A dash of salt, black pepper and cayenne pepper
- 2 Tbsp salsa
- 1 pita bread
- 1 tomato, diced
- 1/2 cup shredded lettuce
- 1/4 cup avocado, sliced
- 1 Tbsp low fat sour cream

Instructions:

1. Slice the chicken breast into strips.

2. Heat a small nonstick frying pan over low-medium and pour in oil. Saute chicken, then add salt, pepper, cayenne pepper, onion powder and garlic powder.

3. Add salsa and let simmer until chicken is completely cooked.

4. Cut pita in half and spoon chicken into pocket. Add tomatoes, lettuce, avocado and sour cream. Enjoy!

Pasta with Swiss Chard

Prep Time: 20 to 25 minutes

Ingredients:

- a handful of Angel's hair pasta (preferably whole wheat)

- 1 Tbsp olive oil

- 1 clove garlic

- 1/2 tsp capers

- 1 small bunch of Swiss chard

- 1 tsp lemon juice

- 1 Tbsp grated Parmesan cheese

Instructions:

1. Chop the Swiss chard and mince the garlic.

2. Fill a small pot with water and add some oil and salt. Let boil over high heat.

3. Add pasta and cook uncovered. Follow manufacturer's instructions as to how long it should be in the pot to get al dente.

4. Drain the pasta and set aside.

5. Heat olive oil in a small nonstick pan over medium. Saute the garlic until translucent, then add Swiss chard and stir until tender. Add a bit of pasta water to help steam and soften the chard.

6. Add the pasta to the olive oil and chard mixture. Add the capers and season with salt and pepper.

7. Transfer to a plate and add lemon juice. Sprinkle Parmesan cheese on top and enjoy!

Chapter 5 - Scrumptious and Healthy Snack and Dessert Recipes

Healthy snacks in between meals is the best way to curb those food cravings and keep that nasty food binge away. Likewise, there is no harm in indulging yourself in a delectable dessert that is just enough for one. Have fun whipping up and digging into these tasty snacks and dessert recipes. If you have a fridge, or if you have some friends over, you can double or even triple the measurements.

Butterscotch Pudding

Prep Time: 10 minutes, 3 hrs freezing time

Ingredients:

- 1/4 cup whole milk
- 1/2 Tbsp cornstarch
- 1/3 cup 2 percent reduced-fat milk
- 1 Tbsp dark brown sugar
- 1/3 tsp vanilla extract
- A pinch of salt
- 1 medium-sized egg yolk
- 1 tsp cold butter

Instructions:

1. Mix some of the whole milk and cornstarch in a bowl using a fork or whisk.

2. Combine the rest of the whole milk with the 2-percent milk in a small pan over medium heat. Let simmer.

3. Add the vanilla extract, brown sugar, salt, and egg yolk to the cornstarch mixture. Mix well. Slowly add the heated milk to the mixture while constantly whisking.

4. Transfer mixture into a small pan and cook over medium heat. Let boil while constantly whisking.

5. Cook mixture until it thickens. Always stir.

6. Remove from heat and stir in butter until it melts.

7. Transfer into a glass or container and place into the fridge or cooler. Cover with plastic wrap and chill for at least 180 minutes before eating.

Peach Mango Smoothie

Prep Time: 5 minutes

Ingredients:

- 1 6-oz container of organic fat-free yogurt
- 1 tsp honey or agave syrup
- 1/4 cup frozen sliced peaches
- 1/4 cup peach nectar
- 1/4 cup frozen mango pieces

Instructions:

Put all of the ingredients in a blender and blend until smooth; or mix together in a bowl for a chunky dessert. Eat immediately after preparing.

Peanut Butter and Banana Rolls

Prep Time: 5 minutes

Ingredients:

- 1 ripe banana
- 1 tsp orange juice
- 2 Tbsp peanut butter
- 1 Tbsp vanilla yogurt
- A dash of ground cinnamon
- 1/2 Tbsp honey-crunch wheat germ

- 1 flour tortilla

Instructions:

1. Mix the peanut butter and yogurt together until smooth.

2. Slice the banana and add orange juice. Coat slices with the juice.

3. Spread the peanut butter and yogurt mixture on the tortilla but leave half an inch of the border uncovered.

4. Place the banana slices on top of the coated tortilla in one layer.

5. Add the cinnamon to the wheat germ and sprinkle over the banana and tortilla.

6. Roll it up and slice into bite-sized pieces. Enjoy!

Recipe Hummus and Veggie Plate

Prep Time: 3 minutes

Ingredients:

- 1 Tbsp hummus (you can buy it from the grocery store; to make your own, see next recipe)
- 1 celery stalk
- 1 carrot or 5 baby carrots
- 1 small cucumber

Instructions:

1. Cut up the carrot, celery stalk and cucumber into bite-sized sticks.

2. Place the hummus in the center of a plate.

3. Arrange the vegetables around the hummus. Dip one veggie stick into the hummus before eating.

Homemade Hummus

Store in the cooler or fridge in an airtight container. Can yield up to 5 servings.

Cooking Books Box Set #17: Cooking for One Cookbook for Beginners & Slow Cooking Guide for Beginners & Wok Cookbook for Beginners

Prep Time: 5 minutes

Ingredients:

- 5 Tbsp water
- 3 Tbsp olive oil
- 1/2 tsp salt
- 2 15-oz cans of chickpeas
- 1 clove garlic
- 1/4 cup freshly squeezed lemon juice
- 1/4 cup roasted sesame seed paste (tahini)
- Optional: 1/2 tsp paprika, freshly chopped flat-leaf parsley, and 1 Tbsp roasted pine nuts

Instructions:

1. Wash and drain chickpeas.

2. Combine water, olive oil, salt, chickpeas, lemon juice, and roasted sesame seed paste in a food processor and process until smooth.

3. Transfer into a container and add paprika, parsley and pine nuts on top.

Pretzels with Peanut Butter and Chocolate Dip

The recipe yields up to 30 pretzels. Keep the pretzels and dip in airtight containers for future snack times.

Prep time: 45 minutes

Ingredients:

- 4 oz. Milk chocolate
- 1/4 cup peanut butter, creamy
- 30 braided pretzel twists (preferably honey-wheat)

Instructions:

1. Place parchment paper on a tray.

2. Put the chocolate in a heat-resistant bowl on top of a small saucepan full of water. Place on medium-high heat to melt the chocolate. Keep stirring throughout the process.

3. Add the peanut butter and stir until combined thoroughly. Turn off the heat.

4. Dip each pretzel into the mixture and place on the parchment paper-lined tray.

5. Place tray in freezer for 30 minutes or cooler for 60 minutes.

Store the rest of the pretzels in an airtight container in the fridge for up to 5 days.

Conclusion

Thank you again for purchasing this book!

I hope this book was able to help you to prepare a healthy meal plan and enjoy delicious good-for-one homemade dishes.

The next step is to try all of the recipes, depending on the equipment and ingredients that are readily available to you. Don't be afraid to experiment with what's in season and to do some more research on recipes for one.

Finally, if you enjoyed this book, please take the time to share your thoughts and post a review on Amazon. We do our best to reach out to readers and provide the best value we can. Your positive review will help us achieve that. It'd be greatly appreciated!

Thank you and good luck!

Book 2:
Slow Cooking Guide for Beginners

By Claire Daniels

The Top Essential Slow Cooking Tips & Recipes for Beginners!

Cooking Books Box Set #17: Cooking for One Cookbook for Beginners & Slow
Cooking Guide for Beginners & Wok Cookbook for Beginners

Table Of Contents

Introduction

I want to thank you and congratulate you for purchasing the book, *"Slow Cooking Guide for Beginners: The Top Essential Slow Cooking Tips and Recipes for Beginners"*.

This book contains proven steps and strategies on how to use your slow cooker in creating delicious dishes for you and your family to enjoy.

All the recipes found in this ebook may look intimidating especially with the amount of ingredients needed. But don't be fooled. These recipes are very easy to do and require less effort than when you're cooking in the stove.

Thanks again for purchasing this book, I hope you enjoy it!

Chapter 1: Slow Cooking and Slow Cookers

We live in a fast paced world. We want everything easy and quick especially in preparing delicious meals for our family. But sometimes, going slow can be quite advantageous.

Slow cooking is a cooking method that utilizes low heat for an extended period of time. The food prepared using this method will become oh-so-tender and more flavorful. In the past, slow cooking involves putting a pot in the stove over a low fire for several hours. Unfortunately, this leaves room for the homemaker to do anything else since the flame needs constant supervision. If not, the pot may over boil, dry out, and cause a fire if left on for too long even on low. Fortunately, this won't be an issue anymore since the slow cooker has already been invented.

The Slow Cooker

The slow cooker, also known as a crockpot, is a special electric pot with a glass lid and inset ceramic bowl. It typically has two temperature settings such as low (180°F to 200°F) and high (280°F to 300°F). It uses indirect heat to cook food in a steady and moderated temperature that doesn't result in food, or worse, house burning even when left on for most of the day.

You can turn it on it on the morning before you leave for work and come home to a warm and perfectly cooked dish. You may also turn it on before sleeping at night so you'll get to enjoy a delicious meal as soon as you wake up.

There are many advantages to owning a slow cooker. Here are some of them:

1. Most slow cooker dish recipes don't have a lot complicated steps involved. In fact, some recipes just require you to dump all the pre-measured and pre-cut ingredients in the pot, cover the lid, and voila! A tasty dish is made. Not much effort and zero hassle.

2. It doesn't use gas and is very energy-efficient. Most slow cooker units even have a power-saving feature that automatically turns off after the desired number of hours.

3. It stretches the family budget since cheaper cuts of tough meat can be made tender and delicious. It also softens even the most fibrous vegetables.

4. It makes a great summer cooking equipment since it doesn't heat up the whole house as an oven or stove.

5. It keeps the prepared food warm to allow family members to eat a warm meal even at different times if necessary.

34

6. Since it uses indirect, low heat, thick stews, bean chili, and other similar dishes won't stick to the bottom of the pot compared to when it's cooked using a stove. No stirring necessary.

7. Since it doesn't need any tending or special attention, you can focus on creating other complicated dishes if ever you'll be entertaining guests at your home. If you aren't cooking anything else, you can just focus on cleaning the house, setting the table, and other chores.

Choosing the Right Slow Cooker

Slow cookers are very common in today's market. The units are available in different designs and sizes. Some brands may be more expensive than others but this may be because of some features that the manufacturer added into the unit.

The best slow cooker that you can own is the one that suits your cooking needs and your budget. Because of the vast array of choices, you'll surely find the slow cooker that meets your criteria.

Here are some things to consider when buying your own slow cooker:

- How many slow cookers are you going to buy? If you're going to splurge and buy two units, you can choose a large and a small unit. Small 1 quart slow cookers are perfect for keeping dips and fondues warm for hours during a party. Large 6 quart units are perfect for slow cooking large cuts of meats and producing large quantities of food for a big family. If you are buying only one unit, choose between a medium sized 4 quart slow cooker and a large 6 quart one.

  Note: All the recipes in this wonderful ebook require a large slow cooker.

- Slow cooker pots can either be round or oval. Oval shaped pots are able to accommodate larger pieces of meat while round pots are great for evenly cooking desserts and cakes.

- Make sure that your slow cooker of choice comes with a programmable timer that lets you cook your food from 30 minutes up to 15 or 20 hours. Also, check if the slow cooker shifts to an automatic off or warm function once the allotted cooking time is over.

There are many slow cookers in the market today. However, some units are not what they claim to be. If the so-called slow cooker comes with a metal insert, not ceramic or earthenware, this means that it cooks with direct heat. These fake slow cookers don't have the same assembly structure and parts as an authentic slow cooker then it won't cook as similarly too.

Cooking with Slow Cookers

- Slow cookers require electricity. In case a power interruption happens while you're cooking, don't fret. You can easily finish cooking the food using your gas oven or stove. Or you can rush your slow cooker over to a friend's house to resume cooking.

- Conventional cooking time is about quadruple on low and double on high when cooking with slow cookers.

- Place the vegetables at the bottom of the slow cooker. You'll be surprised to find out that they cook much longer than the meat.

- Some slow cooker recipes require browning of meat in a pan before placing in the slow cooker. This step is essential since the meat flavors are locked in and makes the dish more visually appetizing.

- When your dish is already in the slow cooker, never stir or remove the lid unless the directions call for it.

Chapter 2: Dips and Sauces Recipes

Spaghetti Bolognese Sauce

Makes 4 servings

Ingredients:

1 lb lean ground beef chuck, 2 carrots (chopped finely), 1 celery stalk (chopped), 1 onion (chopped), 1 can (28 ounces) whole peeled tomatoes (including juice), ¼ c tomato paste, 1 tsp dried thyme, 1 tsp dried oregano, 1 tsp dried basil, 1 bay leaf, ¼ c dry red wine, 1 tsp kosher salt, ½ tsp freshly ground pepper

Directions:

1. Place beef, carrots, celery, onion, garlic, tomato paste, canned tomatoes, oregano, basil, bay leaf, thyme, wine, salt and pepper in the bottom of the slow cooker. Mix well to incorporate.

2. Cover your slow cooker and cook on high for 4 to 5 hours, or low for 7 to 8 hours

3. Serve with a cooked pasta and fresh parmesan on top.

*this Bolognese recipe can be doubled/tripled and frozen for later use.

Spicy Beef Chili

Makes 6 servings

Ingredients:

2 lbs lean ground beef, 1 can (28 ounces) diced tomatoes, 1 can (14 ounces) tomato sauce, 2 cans kidney beans (15 ounces each, drained and rinsed), 3 tbsp olive oil, 6 garlic cloves (finely chopped) 1 red bell pepper (diced), 2 yellow onions (diced), 1 tbsp ground cumin, ¼ c chili powder, 1 ½ tsp kosher salt, and ¼ c pickled jalapeños (drained and chopped)

Directions:

1. Heat the oil in a skillet over medium-high fire. Sauté the bell pepper and onions. Season lightly with salt. Add the garlic, cumin, and chili powder.

2. Add the ground beef and season with a bit of salt if you prefer. Break the meat into smaller pieces and cook until browned.

3. Transfer the beef mixture to your slow cooker. Add the tomatoes and its juice, beans, and tomato sauce. Stir well.

4. Cover your slow cooker and cook for about 6 hours on low.

5. Stir in the jalapeños. Season some more if still needed.

6. Serve warm with sour cream and cheese.

*omit jalapenos if you prefer a mild chili. This recipe can also be frozen

Spinach Parmesan Dip

Makes 16 servings

Ingredients:

2 packages (10 ounces each) frozen spinach (thawed and chopped), 1 can (14 ounces) artichoke hearts (drained and chopped), 1 onion (chopped), 4 garlic cloves (minced), 1 tbsp Dijon mustard, ¼ teaspoon cayenne pepper, ½ c light mayonnaise, ¼ c parmesan cheese (shredded), 1 tbsp lemon juice, ½ c sour cream (fat free), and ¼ c Italian cheese blend (shredded)

Directions:

1. Coat your slow cooker pot with cooking spray.

2. Squeeze any liquids out of your spinach. Reserve the liquid.

3. Put the spinach, onion, artichoke hearts, mustard, garlic, and pepper. Add in the 1/3 cup of the spinach liquid. Stir well.

4. Cover your slow cooker and cook for 3 hours on low.

5. Turn off your slow cooker. Remove the lid and add in the mayonnaise, parmesan cheese, sour cream, lemon juice, and Italian cheese blend. Stir well.

6. Serve immediately with pita chips, sourdough bread or crackers

Apple Butter

Makes 4 cups

Ingredients:

10 apples (peeled and cut into chunks), 1 packed c brown sugar, ¼ c apple cider, ½ c honey, ¼ tsp ground cloves, 1 tbsp ground cinnamon

Directions:

1. Combine all your ingredients in your slow cooker.

2. Place the lid and cook for 10 hours on low.

3. Once cooked, take a fine mesh sieve and place it over a large bowl.

4. Take a cup (or less if the sieve is small) of the apple mixture and put it in the sieve. Use the back of a spoon to push the mixture through the sieve and into the bowl.

5. Repeat the entire process with the remaining apple mixture.

6. Put back the sieved apple mixture into the slow cooker and cook, without the lid on, for 1 ½ hours on high.

7. Once the mixture is thick, stir several times and remove from the heat.

8. Serve warm with toast, muffins, ice cream or pork chops. Store any leftovers in an airtight container, refrigerated for up to a week

Queso Verde

Makes 22 servings (1/4 cup each)

Ingredients:

1 lb ground turkey (uncooked), 1 tbsp cooking oil, ¾ c onion (chopped), 1 jar (16 ounces) salsa verde, 2 c Monterey Jack cheese (shredded), 1 package (8 ounces) cream cheese, 1 tbsp Worcestershire chicken marinade, 1 poblano pepper (seeded and chopped), 2 garlic cloves (minced), 1 tsp ground cumin, 1 tbsp fresh cilantro (chopped)

Directions:

1. Using a skillet, heat the oil over medium heat and cook the onion and ground turkey. Cook until the turkey is slightly browned. Drain fat.

2. Put the cooked turkey mixture in your slow cooker and put in the Monterey Jack cheese, cream cheese, salsa, poblano pepper, Worcestershire marinade, garlic and cumin. Mix well.

3. Cover your slow cooker and cook for 3 ½ hours on low.

4. Once finished cooking, remove the lid and stir to blend the cheeses. Sprinkle the cilantro on top.

5. Replace cover and let warm for 2 more minutes before serving.

6. Serve warm with tortilla chips.

Chapter 3: Meat Dish Recipes

Lamb Tagine with Olives and Apricots

Makes 4 servings

Ingredients:

1 ½ lbs lamb shoulder (cut into 1-inch pieces), ½ c green olives (pitted), ½ c
dried apricots (halved), 1 onion (chopped), 4 carrots (sliced thickly), 2 garlic
cloves (chopped), 1 tsp ground cumin, 1 tsp paprika, ½ tsp ground ginger, ½ tsp
ground cinnamon, 2 tbsp all-purpose flour, 2 tbsp olive oil, 2 tsp kosher salt, and
½ tsp freshly ground pepper

Directions:

1. Heat the olive oil in a skillet over a medium-high flame.

2. Season the lamb with ½ tsp pepper and 1 sp salt.

3. Cooking in small batches brown lamb on all sides.

4. Transfer the cooked lamb to the slow cooker.

5. Place the carrots, onions, olives, apricots, paprika, cinnamon, flour, garlic,
   cumin, ginger, 1 tsp salt, and ½ c water

6. Cover your slow cooker and cook for 8 hours on low.

7. Serve warm with couscous and green salad.

Bratwurst with Potatoes and Sauerkraut

Makes 4 servings

Ingredients:

1 ½ lbs bratwurst links, 1 ½ lbs red new potatoes (scrubbed and halved), 2 c
sauerkraut (drained), 1 tsp caraway seeds, 1 onion (sliced thinly), ½ c chicken
broth (low sodium), ¼ c white wine, and ¼ c fresh flat-leaf parsley (chopped), ¼
tsp freshly ground pepper, and ½ tsp kosher salt

Directions:

1. Place the sauerkraut, potatoes, onions, wine, broth, caraway seeds, salt
   and pepper in your slow cooker. Mix well and spread evenly around the
   bottom of the cooker.

2. Place the bratwurst links on top of the vegetables.

3. Cover the slow cooker and cook for 8-9 hours on low.

4. Sprinkle with parsley on top and serve immediately.

Pulled Pork Sandwiches

Makes 9-10 servings

Ingredients:

1 pork butt roast (about 4 lbs), 2 onions (sliced), 1 jar (16 ounces) of your favorite barbecue sauce, 1 tsp kosher salt, ½ tsp freshly ground pepper

Directions:

1. Trim any excess fat from your pork butt. Season entirely with salt and pepper. Set aside.

2. Put the sliced onions in the slow cooker. Spread evenly in the bottom.

3. Place the meat on top. If your slow cooker is small, you may cut the meat in half and arrange accordingly.

4. Pour 1 c of the barbecue sauce over the meat. Flip it over to fully coat it with sauce.

5. Cover your slow cooker and cook for 10 hours on low.

6. Once the meat is tender, remove from the slow cooker. Put in a large dish or baking tray.

7. Strain the juices and fat but retain the onions inside the slow cooker.

8. Using two forks, shred the pork butt roast into chunks. Discard any fat you find.

9. Put back the chunks of meat, juices included, into the slow cooker.

10. Mix in the remaining barbecue sauce and let cook in low setting for another hour.

11. Serve the meat chunks in soft rolls with the onions as a side dish.

Asian Style Braised Beef Short-Ribs

Makes 4 servings

Ingredients:

3 lbs beef short ribs, 2 tbsp olive oil, ½ tsp sesame oil, 1 carrot (sliced), 1 onion (chopped), 1 packed c brown sugar, 2 c low sodium beef stock, ½ c rice wine vinegar, 1 c low sodium soy sauce, 5 garlic cloves, 3 spring onions (sliced)

Directions:

1. Heat the olive oil in a pan over medium heat.

2. Season the beef with salt and pepper. Cook in batches, browning the beef on all sides. Remove from the pan and set aside.

3. Put the carrot, onion, sugar, soy sauce, stock, vinegar, garlic, sesame oil. Mix well.

4. Put the beef into the slow cooker. Spread evenly.

5. Cover your slow cooker and cook on low for 8 hours.

6. Serve warm over white rice and the broccoli on the side. Top with red chili and spring onion slices.

Corned Beef and Cabbage

Makes 4-5 servings

Ingredients:

4 lbs corned beef brisket (rinsed and pat dried), 6 carrots (peeled and sliced), 6 potatoes (peeled and quartered), 1 head cabbage (cut into wedges), 1 onion (cut into wedges), 1 bay leaf, 2 garlic cloves (minced), 2 tsp brown sugar, 1 bottle of Dark Beer (Such as Guinness), and a dash of whole cloves.

Directions:

1. Coat the insides of your slow cooker with cooking spray or oil.

2. Place the onion, carrots, and potatoes in your slow cooker.

3. In small bowl, combine the brown sugar and the clove. Stir well.

4. Rub the beef with sugar and clove mixture.

5. Place the meat on top of the vegetables in the crockpot.

6. Add the bay leaf and garlic.

7. Pour the beer all over the meat and vegetables.

8. Cover the slow cooker and cook for 9 to 10 hours on low.

9. 1 hour before the cooking time ends, add the cabbage wedges.

10. Continue cooking until the cabbage is somewhat tender.

11. Remove the bay leaf and serve.

Chapter 4: Seafood & Vegetable Dish Recipes

Greek Salmon Bake

Makes 4-5 servings

Ingredients:

30 ounces salmon fillets, 1 can (15 ounces) tomatoes, 1 can (10.75 ounces) cream of onion soup, 4 eggs (beaten), 4 c bread crumbs, 1 green bell pepper (chopped), 1 tsp Greek seasoning, 2 chicken bouillon cubes (crushed), 1 tsp fresh lemon juice, 1 tsp garlic powder, 1 can (10.75 ounces) cream of celery soup, ¼ c milk

Directions:

1. Line your slow cooker with a greased slow cooker liner.

2. Arrange the salmon pieces at the bottom of your slow cooker.

3. Using a mixing bowl, combine all the ingredients except for the milk and celery soup. Stir well.

4. Carefully, transfer the mixture into your slow cooker and over the salmon fillets.

5. Cover the slow cooker and cook for 5 hours on low.

6. Once the salmon is done, prepare the creamy topping by combining the celery soup and milk in a saucepan. Bring to a boil over medium heat until thick.

7. Transfer the salmon into a serving dish on a bed of cooked rice pilaf.

8. Serve warm with a creamy celery sauce on top.

Fast and Easy Garlic Shrimp

Makes 6-8 servings

Ingredients:

2 lbs extra large shrimp (raw, peeled, and de-veined), 6 garlic cloves (sliced thinly), ¾ c extra virgin olive oil, 1 tsp smoked Spanish paprika, ¼ tsp freshly ground pepper, 1 tsp kosher salt, ¼ tsp red pepper flakes (crushed)

Directions:

1. Combine the oil, salt, black pepper, garlic, paprika, and red pepper flakes in your slow cooker. Stir well.

2. Cover your slow cooker and cook on high.

3. After 30 minutes, put your shrimp in the slow cooker. Stir to coat evenly.

4. Replace your slow cooker's lid and cook for 10 minutes on high or until the shrimp turn opaque.

5. Place into a shallow serving dish and top with more of the sauce.

6. Serve immediately.

Slow Cooked Cream of Crab Soup

Makes 4 servings

Ingredients:

2 c fresh crabmeat (picked and flaked), 2 c half and half, 2 c milk, 2 fresh lemon peel (cut into strips), ½ tsp ground mace, 3 tbsp butter, ½ c saltine crackers (crumbs), and 2 tbsp dry sherry

Directions:

1. Combine all the ingredients in your slow cooker except the dry sherry and saltine crackers. Stir well.

2. Cover your slow cooker and cook for 4 to 5 hours on low.

3. Before serving, put in the saltine cracker crumbs and sherry. Stir well to thicken the soup.

4. Serve immediately.

Italian-Style Seafood Stew

Makes 4 servings

Ingredients:

¾ lbs fresh snapper fillet (cubed), 16 prawns (large and peeled with tail intact), 16 fresh mussels, 1 onion (diced finely), ½ green bell pepper (diced finely), 2 garlic cloves (minced), 1 can (28 ounces) diced tomatoes, ¾ c dry white wine, 1 can (10 ounces) clam nectar, 2 tbsp tomato paste, 1 tbsp fresh parsley (chopped), 1 tsp dried oregano, ½ tsp freshly ground black pepper and pinch of dried thyme.

Directions:

Cooking Books Box Set #17: Cooking for One Cookbook for Beginners & Slow Cooking Guide for Beginners & Wok Cookbook for Beginners

1. Combine the onions, bell pepper, garlic, oregano, thyme, tomato paste, diced tomatoes, white wine, clam nectar and black pepper in your slow cooker. Stir well.

2. Cover your slow cooker and cook for 4 hours on low.

3. After the appropriate time, stir in the mussels, prawns, and snapper.

4. Replace the lid and cook for 15 minutes more or until the fish is cooked and the mussels are open.

5. Serve warm with fresh parsley garnish.

Chapter 5: Poultry Dish Recipes

Chicken A la King

Makes 6-8 servings

Ingredients:

3 c cooked chicken (cut into cubes), ¼ c onions (chopped finely), ¼ c green pepper (chopped finely), ¼ c celery (chopped finely), 1 can button mushrooms (4 ounces, drained), ¼ c pimiento olives (chopped), 1 can (10 ounces) cream of mushroom soup, 1 can (13 ounces) evaporated milk, 1/8 tsp freshly ground pepper, and ½ tsp kosher salt

Directions:

1. Put all the ingredients in your slow cooker. Mix well.

2. Cover your slow cooker and cook for 2 to 3 hours on low.

3. Serve warm over white rice.

Classic Chicken and Dumplings

Makes 7-8 servings

Ingredients:

6 chicken breast halves (skinless, boneless), 2 c baby carrots, 2 Yukon gold potatoes (sliced into 1-inch pieces), 2 celery stalks (sliced), 2 c all purpose flour, 2 cans condensed cream of chicken soup (10 ¾ ounces each),2/3 c milk, ¼ tsp freshly ground black pepper, and 1 tsp dried thyme leaves (crushed),

Directions:

1. Wash the chicken breasts. Cut into 1-inch pieces. Put in your slow cooker.

2. Add in the carrots, potatoes, and celery.

3. Using a small bowl, combine the black pepper, thyme, water and soup. Stir well. Pour over the chicken and vegetables.

4. Cover the slow cooker and cook on low for 8 hours.

5. After 8 hours, combine the milk and flour in a bowl. Stir well to dissolve any lumps.

6. Carefully, drop spoonfuls of the batter into the chicken mixture. Close the lid and change the setting to high.

7. Let the dumplings cook for another 4 hours.

8. Serve hot.

Spicy Sesame Honey Chicken

Makes 3 servings

Ingredients:

1 lb chicken breasts (skinless and boneless), 1 garlic clove (minced), 2 tbsp diced onion, ¼ c low sodium soy sauce, ½ c honey, 1 tbsp olive oil, 2 tbsp ketchup, 6 tbsp water, 2 tsp cornstarch, ¼ tsp red pepper flakes and sesame seeds

Directions:

1. Lightly season all sides of the chicken with salt and pepper. Arrange the chicken in your slow cooker.

2. In a small bowl, combine the soy sauce, honey, ketchup, oil, pepper flakes, garlic, and onion. Mix well. Pour the mixture evenly over the chicken.

3. Cover the slow cooker and cook for 4 hours on low.

4. Once the chicken is cooked, remove the chicken from the crockpot and transfer to a serving dish. Retain the sauce.

5. Dissolve the cornstarch in the water and stir well to remove any lumps.

6. Add the cornstarch mixture into the sauce and stir to thicken.

7. Cover the slow cooker and let the sauce cook for 10 minutes.

8. Slice chicken into bite size pieces and put back into the slow cooker. Mix to coat the chicken with sauce.

9. Serve warm over rice and sesame seeds sprinkled to garnish.

Soy-Glazed Chicken with Stir-Fried Vegetables Siding

Makes 4 servings

Ingredients:

1 ½ lbs chicken thighs (boneless and skinless), ½ c packed light brown sugar, 3 tbsp fresh lemon juice, 3 tbsp low sodium soy sauce, 2 tbsp fish sauce, ¼ tsp crushed red pepper, 1 tbsp fresh ginger root (grated), 1 tbsp olive oil, 2 heads baby bok choy (leaves separated), 4 scallions (chopped), 1 red bell pepper (sliced

into strips), 2 garlic cloves (sliced thinly), ¾ lbs snow peas (trimmed), and ¼ tsp freshly ground black pepper

Directions:

1. Pour the sugar, lemon juice, soy sauce, ginger, fish sauce, and crushed red pepper into your slow cooker. Stir well.

2. Add the chicken and turn several times to coat evenly.

3. Cover your slow cooker and cook for 4 to 5 hours on high.

4. Once cooked, transfer the chicken into a serving plate. Keep warm.

5. Pour the chicken's cooking liquid into a skillet. Let simmer in low heat until thickened. Prepare the stir-fried vegetables.

6. Heat the oil in another skillet or wok over medium-high heat. Add the garlic, bok choy, scallions, snow peas, and bell pepper. Toss frequently until the vegetables are tender. Season with black pepper.

7. Drizzle the thickened sauce over the chicken.

8. Serve the chicken with the stir-fried vegetables on the side.

Chapter 6: Dessert & Snack Recipes

Walnut Maple Pudding

Makes 5 servings

Ingredients:

¾ c pure maple syrup, 1 c walnuts (chopped), 1 ¾ c whole milk, 3 eggs, 1 ½ tsp ground cinnamon, 6 tbsp butter (unsalted, melted), 1 ½ tsp pure vanilla extract, 5 c egg bread of your choice (cubed), pinch of kosher salt

Directions:

1. Preheat your oven to 350°F. Generously coat the insides of your slow cooker with butter or cooking spray.

2. Place walnuts on a baking sheet and bake for 5 minutes or until lightly brown. Remove from the oven and set aside.

3. In a mixing bowl, combine the milk, maple syrup, and eggs. Whisk well. Add the melted butter, salt, cinnamon, and vanilla extract.

4. Place the cubed bread into the liquids and press down until the maple mixture is fully absorbed.

5. Carefully, transfer the bread into your slow cooker.

6. Place the lid and cook on high for 2 to 3 hours or until an inserted toothpick comes out clean.

7. Serve warm with vanilla ice cream

Apple Crumble

Makes 4- 6 servings

Ingredients:

2 l apples (peeled, cored, and sliced thinly), 2 tbsp + 6 tbsp unsalted butter, ¼ c granulated sugar, 2 tbsp fresh lemon juice, 2 tbsp all-purpose flour, 13/4 c quick oats, ½ tsp+ ½ tsp ground cinnamon, and ½ firmly packed cup dark brown sugar

Directions:

1. Melt the 6 tbsp of butter and set aside. Cut the remaining butter into small chunks.

2. Put the apples in the slow cooker and drizzle with lemon juice. Mix.

3. Using a small bowl, combine the flour, ½ tsp cinnamon, and granulated sugar. Mix well. Pour over the apples and mix well to coat.

4. Arrange the apples in an even layer at the bottom of the slow cooker.

5. Spread the small butter chunks on top of the apples.

6. Using another bowl, mix the remaining cinnamon, brown sugar, oats, and melted butter. Stir well.

7. Pour the oat mixture evenly over the apples.

8. Cover the slow cooker and cook for 4 hours on low.

9. Serve warm with whipped cream or ice cream

Mocha Coconut Poached Pears

Ingredients:

6 fresh pears (ripe but firm, peeled), 2 tbsp cocoa powder (unsweetened), ¼ c sugar, 1/3 c strong coffee, 2/3 c light coconut milk (unsweetened), 2 tbsp coffee liqueur

Directions:

1. Cut the pears into quarters, lengthwise.

2. Arrange the pears at the bottom of your slow cooker.

3. Using a bowl, combine the cocoa powder and sugar. Add in the coffee, coffee liqueur, and coconut milk. Stir well. Pour the mixture over the pears.

4. Cover your slow cooker and cook for 4 hours on low.

5. Transfer the pears to a serving dish using a slotted spoon.

6. Serve with coconut toasted coconut shreds or grated chocolate on top.

Orange Ginger Cheesecake

*for round pot slow cookers

Makes 10 servings

Ingredients:

12 ounces cream cheese (reduced fat, softened), 2 blood oranges (sliced), 3 eggs (lightly beaten), ½ c sugar, 2 tbsp orange juice, 1 tsp freshly shredded orange peel, ½ tsp vanilla, 1 tbsp all-purpose flour, ½ c non fat sour cream, 1 c warm water, and crystalized ginger (finely chopped)

Directions:

1. Prepare a 1 ½ quart soufflé dish. Lightly coat it with cooking spray.

2. Cut on an 18x12 inch heavy foil. Cut into half lengthwise. Fold the halves into thirds lengthwise. Crisscross the strips of foil and position the soufflé dish in the center.

3. Using an electric mixer, combine the sugar, cream cheese, orange juice, vanilla, and flour on medium speed.

4. Once well-combined, beat in the sour cream until a smooth consistency is achieved.

5. Stir in the orange peel and mix well. Pour the mixture into the soufflé dish. Level with a spatula.

6. Cover the soufflé dish tightly with the foil strips. Set aside.

7. Pour the warm water into your slow cooker. Transfer the soufflé dish into the slow cooker. Don't remove the foil strips.

8. Cover the slow cooker and cook for 2 ½ hours on high.

9. Once the center is set, carefully removed the soufflé dish using the foil strips.

10. Remove the foil strips and let the dish cool.

11. Once room temperature, cover the soufflé dish and chill for 24 hours before serving.

12. Serve with blood orange slices and ginger on top.

Conclusion

Thank you again for purchasing this book!

I hope this book was able to help you to overcome your hesitation in using the slow cooker as your primary cooking equipment at home. I hope that you enjoyed all the recipes and will continue making them for many years to come.

The next step is to produce your own unique slow cooker recipes that you can pass on to your friends, daughters, and sons. So don't stop experimenting with various ingredients in your slow cooker.

Finally, if you enjoyed this book, please take the time to share your thoughts and post a review on Amazon. We do our best to reach out to readers and provide the best value we can. Your positive review will help us achieve that. It'd be greatly appreciated!

Thank you and good luck!

Book 3:

Wok Cookbook for Beginners:

By Claire Daniels

The Top Easy and Quick Recipes for Wok Cooking For Beginners!

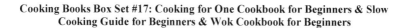

Copyright 2014 by Claire Daniels - All rights reserved.

Table Of Contents

Introduction

I want to thank you and congratulate you for purchasing the book, *"Wok Cookbook for Beginners: The Top Easy and Quick Recipes for Wok Cooking For Beginners!".*

This book contains proven steps and strategies on how to cook delicious meals using your wok.

Basically, the book has three chapters. The first one tackles the general tips that you need to know when using the wok. The second chapter, the heart and soul of this compendium, contains the easiest wok recipes. Finally, the tips on how to clean your wok are discussed in the third and final chapter.

Thanks again for purchasing this book, I hope you enjoy it!

Chapter 1 – General Wok Cooking Tips

Before we jump into any particular recipe, you need to get the hang of using your wok first. Usually, the wok is used for stir-frying. Therefore, you need to learn how to stir-fry. Aside from being delicious, what is it with stir-frying that you would want to learn how to do it?

First and foremost, stir-fried meals are delicious. Aside from that, the resulting meals can be prepared fast. The meals are also really healthy and seasoned. Stir-frying with the use of a wok leads to the creation of meals that can lead to the creation of beautiful works of art in the form of good food. This method is best suited for making meals for one or two people. But if you will choose to cook meals for many people, this can be used, too.

Many people see the wok as an unattractive ornament in the kitchen. This notion is common among people who are not aware of the kinds of dishes that can be made from it. But many people are attracted instantly to have one once they tasted the dishes for themselves. Woks are essential for cooking authentic tasting dishes.

Here are some tips that are worth remembering:

- It is worth purchasing your very own carbon steel wok instead of deep sauté pan. Aside from being very affordable, they are very versatile as well.

- Woks made up of carbon steel will have to undergo seasoning. The process of seasoning is not really difficult. This process can help your wok become better looking. It can also make your nonstick.

- The steps in the subsequent chapter may appear to be intimidating. But with consistent practice, you will find out that cooking in a wok is fun and fulfilling. Learn the recipes that follow by heart and be proud of the meals that you are about to produce.

Chapter 2 – Easy Wok Recipes

Wok Recipe #1: Stir-Fried Ramen

This meal will serve one to two people. The following are the ingredients that you need to prepare: classic ramen noodles and flavor, 2 tablespoons of wok oil, 1/3 cups of onions cut into strips, 1/3 cup of cabbage cut into strips, and 1/3 carrots cut into strips.

First, you need to cook the ramen noodles using the directions given in the package. Drain it and set it aside for a while. The wok oil should be heated up in a frying pan. Once hot, you may add the onions, followed by cabbage and the carrot strips. Once the veggies are cooked to perfection, you may add the noodles and stir it constantly. Upon heating the noodles, add the packet of flavoring. Stir the resulting ramen.

Wok Recipe #2: Shanghai Noodles stirred in a wok with Haricots Verts and Shrimps

This meal can be prepared in one hour, forty-five minutes for preparation and 15 minutes actual cooking. This recipe serves four to six people.

The following are the ingredients that you have to prepare: 1 pound of blanched and refreshed shanghai noodles (the one made out of eggs), ¾ pounds of blanched and refreshed haricots verts, 1 pound of rock shrimp, 1 tablespoon of cornstarch, 1 teaspoon of sesame seed oil, 1 teaspoon of coarse ground coriander seed, 1 tablespoon of minced garlic, 1 tablespoon of minced ginger, 1 piece of sliced red onion, ½ cup of sliced rehydrated black mushrooms, ½ cup of chicken stock, ¼ cup of oyster sauce, some canola oil, and black pepper and salt to taste.

Mix your shrimp, coriander, cornstarch, and sesame oil in a bowl. In a heated wok that is covered with just enough canola oil, you need to stir fry your shrimp for around two minutes until medium rare. The shrimp has to be set aside. In the wok, you need to add a little more canola oil so that you can caramelize your garlic, onions, and garlic. Then, you may season according to preferred taste. Then, you can add oyster sauce, chicken stock, and mushrooms. After that, you may add the noodles, the haricots, and the shrimp. Heat up as quickly as possible and serve immediately.

Wok Recipe #3: Noodles cooked in the Wok Stirred with New Year Veggies

This dish is traditionally served to represent long and unbroken life. It is traditionally eaten during the celebration of Chinese New year for good luck.

The following are the ingredients that you have to prepare: 1 tablespoon of vegetable oil and a bit more that will be used for frying, six to eight slices (around 1/8 of an inch thick) of lotus root, 1 teaspoon of chopped garlic, 1 teaspoon of finely-chopped ginger, 2 ½ ounces of Chinese celery that has been julienned into 1 ½ inches long pieces, 2 ounces of yellow leeks cut into 1 ½ inches long pieces, 2 ounces of sliced shiitake mushroom caps, 2 ounces of black trumpet mushrooms, 2 ounces of snow peas, julienned, 1 tablespoon of Shao Hsing wine, ¼ cups of chicken broth, 1 tablespoon of oyster sauce, ½ teaspoons of sugar, ¼ teaspoon of coarse salt, 8 ounces of e-fu noodles that has been reconstituted according to the directions of the package, 3 drops of white truffle oil, 8 to ten pieces of scallions that has been julienned carefully picked to include only the light green and white parts.

The wok filled with vegetable oil has to be heated until the temperature reaches 250 degrees Fahrenheit. The lotus root can then be added and fried until golden brown. This can be transferred to another bowl. You can wipe off the excess oil using the paper towel.

Then, you can heat another teaspoon of vegetable oil in a wok. Use high heat to cook your ginger and garlic until they are golden brown. Next, you need to add leeks, celery, mushrooms, broth, wine, and snow peas. You can proceed with cooking by stirring for the next thirty seconds. The mixture has to be transferred to a medium sized bowl. You can set the veggie mixture aside.

You may add chicken broth, salt, sugar, and oyster sauce to the pan. Then, you will need to add the noodles to cook. Toss the mixture constantly until all the liquid component of the mixture is absorbed. Let stand for about 1 minute. Return the veggies to the mixture and allow cooking. Aid this with constant stirring. Before removing from the heat, add truffle oil.

Serve while hot. You have the option to garnish your dish with scallions and the previously fried lotus root.

Wok Recipe #4: Scallop Salad in a Wok

The following are the ingredients that you need to prepare: 2 cups of fresh peas (sugar snap variety), 2 cups of spinach, 1 can (8 oz.) of water chestnuts, 2 pieces of shredded carrots, ¼ cup of olive oil, 1 pound of bay scallops, 1 tablespoon of tamari, 2 tablespoons of plum wine, 1 ½ tablespoons of sesame oil, 1 tablespoon of rice wine vinegar, 1 tablespoon of fresh ginger that is minced, and 1 ½ teaspoons of minced garlic.

First, you have to cook the peas in water that is already in full boil. Cover this for half a minute. To stop the process of cooking, drain and put water with ice. Then, you can add in the spinach, peas, shredded carrots, and water chestnuts into a large bowl. For a while, you can set this aside. The scallops can be cooked in hot olive oil using your wok. Use high fire in doing so. Turn the scallops once. Set this aside. Then, you can combine the tamari to the other ingredients. The vegetable can be drizzled over and tossed gently. You may top this with scallops.

Wok Recipe #5: Duck Fried in Oyster Sauce in a Wok

The skin of the duck should be properly scored. Place the duck with skin side down. Put it in a wok. Now, you may turn on the fire. Set it to high. Allow the duck to warm up slowly. By doing so, you will be able to extract the fat contained by the skin. By doing this for the next ten minutes, you will get a better flavor and texture.

On the other hand, you can boil a pot of water. Then, you can put in a dash of oyster sauce to the boiling water. Next, boil the pechay for around two minutes until it is wilted. Drain this and set this aside. Put the fire to low and cook for a few minutes more. After a while, remove the contents from the wok. Allow the duck to cool until it is cool enough to be handled and sliced thinly.

Pour 1 tablespoon of fat from the duck into the wok with the oil. Place the wok into high heat. Put the duck into the hot duck fat. Allow this to cook for the next three minutes until the duck is golden brown. Add pechay and oyster sauce. Simmer the mixture for around two minutes. Serve this while hot.

Wok Recipe #6: Wok-Fried Squid with Greens

This dish is very easy to cook. All you need is ten minutes of cooking time. The preparation of the ingredients will take you around the same time, too. This dish serves two to four people.

The following are the ingredients that you need to prepare: 2 tablespoons of olive oil, 1 pound of squid (including the tentacles and bodies) thoroughly cleaned and sliced into rings (1/2 inches thick), 1 ½ pounds of green leafy vegetables of choice (e.g. pechay), 2 pieces of finely diced Serrano chili, 3 cloves of garlic that are sliced very thinly, ¾ piece of grated ginger, 2 tablespoons of fish sauce, 2 teaspoons of brown sugar, 2 tablespoons of lime juice, and 1 ounce of basil (approximately three pieces of large stems).

The wok needs to be put on medium fire. Once the wok is hot enough, you may put one tablespoon of olive oil. When the wok is already smoking hot, you can add 1 tablespoon of olive oil. Sauté the greens until they are wilted for about five minutes. Set them aside. You may add more olive oil to the hot wok. Then, you add garlic, Serrano chili, and ginger. You can now add squid. Allow this to cook for around 2 minutes.

Mix the following: lime, brown sugar, and fish sauce. Then, you may add this to the greens that you have cooked earlier. Sauté with the basil leaves until the basil is already wilted. Over barley or brown rice, serve the dish. The barley or brown rice will absorb the juices that resulted from the cooking process.

Wok Recipe #7: Fried French Beans and Carrots in a Wok

It is not right to conclude that just because this is made up of veggies, the resulting dish is no longer tasty. Try this and you will find out that the sweetness given by the carrots and the crunchiness provided by the beans will give you something that is heavenly. This recipe can serve 2 people.

The following are the ingredients for this particular dish: 200 grams of peeled carrots sliced on a particular angle, 200 grams of blanched and trimmed French beans, 1 tablespoon of ground nut oil, 2 cloves of finely chopped garlic, 1 tablespoon of oyster sauce, 1 tablespoon of ginger that is finely grated, 1 tablespoon of light soy sauce, 1 tablespoon of rice vinegar, and for garnishing, some crispy shallots.

This dish is fairly easy to cook. First, you just have to put the oil to the wok and set the fire on high. Then, you can cook the ginger and the garlic. You may cook this for thirty seconds. The carrot can be added and it needs to be cooked for the next sixty seconds. You may add the beans together with the oyster sauce, the soy sauce, and vinegar. Toss this for the next thirty seconds. Serve while hot. You may top this with fried shallot as garnishing.

Wok Recipe #8: Chili Fried Chicken

Note that this recipe serves four people. The following are the ingredients that you need to prepare: 1 pound of chicken breast that has been cut into cubes (1 inch x 1 inch), 1 ½ cups of cornstarch, 2 teaspoons of salt, 1 teaspoon of ground black pepper, 3 cups of peanut oil or any vegetable oil, 8 to 10 pieces of dried chili, 3 cloves of minced garlic, 1 piece of leek sliced thinly (use the white part only).

For the marinade, prepare the following: 2 tablespoons of soy sauce, 2 pieces of egg whites, and 2 tablespoons of dry sherry or Chinese rice wine.

For the sauce, use the following: 2 tablespoons of garlic sauce with chili, 1 tablespoon of soy sauce, 1 tablespoon of water or chicken stock, 1 teaspoon of high quality balsamic vinegar (or more preferably, Chinese black vinegar), 1 teaspoon of cornstarch, and 1 teaspoon of ground Sichuan pepper.

You need to prepare the marinade first. In a bowl, you can mix in the following ingredients: rice wine, soy sauce, and the egg whites. The chicken should be coated with the mixture prepared for the marinade. Allow this to sit for at least ten minutes.

For the sauce, the following ingredients have to be mixed together: mix the soy sauce, the chili garlic sauce, the Chinese black vinegar, the chicken stock, the Sichuan pepper, and the cornstarch. This should be set aside for a while.

In a plate or a large bowl, you can mix the following seasonings: pepper, cornstarch, and salt. The chicken that was coated previously can now be dredged in this mixture. Shake the excess cornstarch off.

Next, you may heat three cups of vegetable oil or peanut oil in the wok. Let the oil heat up until it reaches the temperature of 350 degrees Fahrenheit. Fry the chicken in two to three batches. Fry the first batch of the cubed chicken breasts and fry these until they become golden brown. Make sure that they are cooked thoroughly inside and out. The entire process of frying can be finished within four to five minutes. The chicken can be removed with the use of a strainer to drain the oil. To remove excess oil, allow to drain in paper towels. Now, fry the second batch.

In a heatproof container, drain the oil. Save the oil for discarding. Wipe your wok with the use of a paper towel. If there are brown bits, remove them. However, it is not recommended to wash the wok.

Now, you may reheat the wok using high heat. Put in one tablespoon of oil. Swirl the oil so that the sides and base can be coated. You may add the dried chili to your wok and fry until they begin to blister. Stir-fry the ginger, garlic, and leeks. Now, you can add the sauce. Allow the mixture to thicken by allowing to boil for the next one minute. Finally, add the fried chicken. Toss this for thorough mixing, and the heat can be removed. This can now be immediately served.

Wok Recipe #9: Chicken Curry in a Wok

Note that for this dish to be successful, you have to use high quality curry. Many experts recommend curry in the paste form. This gives more depth and a richer kind of flavor compared to the more common curry in powder form. You need to be sure that you shake the canned coconut milk first because it has the tendency to have the creamy part float.

The following are the ingredients that you need to prepare: ½ teaspoons of vegetable oil, 3.5 pounds of chicken, 1 cup of shallots that are sliced thinly, 3 tablespoons of yellow curry paste (alternately, if you love the curry in powder form, you can use 1 tablespoon of curry powder instead), ½ cup of coconut milk in can (the unsweetened variety), ¾ cups of chicken broth, 2 potatoes that are peeled and quartered (cut into ¼ inch slices), 1 piece of green bell pepper cut into strips, 1 teaspoon of salt, and ¼ teaspoon of ground white pepper.

First, you need to heat a wok until the surface is almost dry. A good indicator for this is when the water beads in the wok vaporize within 2 seconds of contact with the heated surface. Now, you may put in the oil. Add the pieces of chicken with the skin side down. Spread this throughout your wok. For the next three to four minutes, allow this to cook undisturbed. Adjust the heat and make it lower as the color of the chicken turns to brown. With the use of a metal spatula, you may turn the chicken pieces every 3 to 4 minutes. Note that the chicken should not necessarily be thoroughly cooked. Well, not yet. Now, put the chicken on a plate and leave the drippings on the pan.

Next, you may add the shallots to the drippings left in the wok. The drippings are more than enough to cook the shallots. Over medium heat, cook the shallot for approximately two to three minutes until they become soft. Until then, you may add the curry powder or curry paste. Cook and stir until your food is fragrant.

The chicken may now be put back on the wok. Stir this well until the chicken is well-combined with the rest of the shallots. You may now put in the coconut milk and the broth. Over high heat, put the mixture to a boil. Once the boiling point is reached, you may add the salt and pepper, bell pepper, and potatoes. Cover the wok and lower the fire to medium. Simmer the mixture for the next fifteen minutes. Now, you may turn the chicken and allow it to brown. The other ingredients have to be closely monitored too.

Wok Recipe #10: Sweet Potato Wok Pudding

The following are the ingredients that you need to prepare: four cups of raw sweet potatoes that have been grated, 1 1/3 cups of milk, 1 cup of sugar, 3 pieces of beaten eggs, ¾ teaspoons of ground all spice, and ¾ teaspoons of ground cinnamon.

To prepare, you need to begin with combining all the ingredients and mixing them thoroughly. Next, you need to pour then into a greased quiche dish. Place the rack in a wok that is filled with water up to 1 inch just below the rack. The water should be brought to boil and the pudding has to be set on the rack.

The wok has to be covered and heat has to be reduced. Simmer the pudding for the next one hour or so. If you wish to add more water, do so only when necessary.

Remove the dish from the wok. Serve this pudding after five minutes, when it is no longer too hot.

Wok Recipe #11: Salmon Smoked in a Wok

This dish will serve two to three people. The following are the ingredients that you need to prepare: ½ cup of soy sauce, ¼ cup of dry sherry or rice wine, 1 tablespoon of ginger root that has been minced, 2 tablespoons of sugar (granulated), 1 pound of salmon fillet, ½ cup of packed brown sugar, 1/3 cup of uncooked rice, ¼ cup of Oolong tea of the traditional Chinese Black tea, 2 whole star anise, 1 teaspoon of cornstarch, and 4 teaspoons of cold water.

In a large mixing bowl, whisk together the following ingredients: Chinese rice wine, soy sauce, 2 teaspoons of sugar, and minced ginger. This will be your marinade. If you are using a frozen salmon, make sure to thaw it properly first. After thawing, cut the salmon crosswise. It should be cut crosswise into 1-inch strips. Add the marinade and coat the salmon completely. Allow to sit for at least ten minutes.

Use a heavy duty wok for this recipe. Make sure to use a big piece of aluminum foil to line your wok. Allow the foil to hang over the wok's edge. In another bowl, mix the following ingredients: long grain rice, brown sugar, the Chinese Black tea, and the star anise. This will serve as your smoking mixture. Spread the smoking mixture at the bottom of the foil that serves as the lining of the wok.

Now, you may set a round rack around the mixture. It should be approximately an inch on top of the mixture. If needed, the aluminum foils should be scrunched into four balls. These should be placed on top of the mixture such that the wire rack can be properly elevated. The uncovered should be placed on high heat.

Allow it to be there for the next five to eight minutes until smoke begins to appear. The marinated strips of salmon should be placed on top of the wire rack, with the skin side facing downwards. Now, you may cover the wok and lower the heat to medium. Continue the smoking process until the strips of salmon has developed a very deep and very rich color. Do this for around ten to twelve minutes. For the first ten minutes of smoking, never remove the lid for continuous smoking.

If done properly, the salmon after smoking easily flakes. Turn off the heat and remove the wok and place it somewhere cool. Let the setup stand for the next ten minutes or so. In a bowl, mix together cold water and the cornstarch. Mix until it is smooth. Pour the marinade into the saucepan and heat it using medium fire. Bring the marinade to boil. Add the cornstarch mixture there and stir until the sauce thickens. Serve the salmon with a little sauce. It is best eaten with hot cooked rice and stir-fried veggies.

Wok Recipe #12: Wok-Tossed Eel with glass noodles and turmeric

The following are the ingredients that you need to prepare: 50 grams of bean thread vermicelli, 3 pieces of dried wood type of ear mushrooms, ½ teaspoons of curry powder, ½ teaspoons of turmeric, ½ teaspoons of chili flakes, 2 tablespoons of fish sauce, 1 tablespoon of sugar, 2 tablespoons of vegetable oil, 2 minced garlic cloves, ½ diced onion, ½ wedge sliced onion, 400 grams of eel fillets, deboned and sliced into 3 centimeter pieces, some 45 milliliters of coconut milk, 2 tablespoons of peanuts that have been roasted and crushed, 1 handful of herb for rice paddies sliced roughly, some roughly sliced Coriander leaves, 2 chili pieces diced, and soy sauce for the dip.

First, you need to soak the bean thread glass vermicelli in water for around 20 to 30 minutes. After that, the water has to be drained so that you can cut it into 10 centimeter lengths. Put the mushrooms now in another bowl and soak it for around twenty minutes. Slice thinly and drain.

Next, you may combine the following ingredients in another bowl: turmeric, chili flakes, and curry powder. Set this mixture aside for a while. In a separate bowl, combine sugar, 2 tablespoons of water and fish sauce. Mix very well and set it aside.

You may now heat the wok over medium fire. Add the vegetable oil, diced onion, the garlic, and the lemon grass. Stir-fry until the mixture is fragrant. Increase heat until the fire is high. Add the eel and for two minutes, stir-fry the eel. Next, you may add the curry powder. Continue stir-frying for the next minute.

By then, you can already add the vermicelli, the ear mushroom, the onion wedges, and the mixture with the fish sauce. Toss the ingredients really well and pour in the coconut milk. Continue stir frying for the next two minutes.

Finally, garnish with crushed roasted peanuts, coriander, and the rice paddy herbs. This meal is best served hot with cooked rice, and dipping.

Wok Recipe #13: The Real Chinese Fried Rice cooked in a Wok

Note that this recipe serves five to six people. The following are the ingredients that you have to prepare: four cups of rice (the jasmine variety), some wok oil, two to three dashes of ginger that has been grated, 1 whole onion chopped, ¾ cup of chicken stock, 1 ½ teaspoon of sugar, 1 teaspoon of sesame oil, 3 pieces of scrambled eggs, 1 cup of frozen carrot and peas, 2 to three teaspoons of salt, and some soy sauce according to taste.

Get 4 cups of cooked jasmine rice. Set this aside in a cool place or in a refrigerator. Next, you may scramble the eggs in a different pan. Do your best to fold the eggs so that they can be cut into strips.

Heat the wok. Add three to four tablespoons of vegetable oil. Use medium heat only. Now, you may sauté the onion until it is transparent for three minutes or so. Then you can add the frozen carrots and peas followed by soy sauce.

Now, you may add the rice. Make sure that you separate the grains with the use of your fingers. Mix the rice well with the veggies. Add some more vegetable oil and sesame seed oil. Put the ginger, chicken stock, and sugar. Top with the strips of scrambled egg.

Put the heat to high and add preferred amount of soy sauce. Stir-fry until desired consistency is achieved. Do your best to do this using the highest heat level.

Stir-fry until all the liquids evaporated. Add little amount of salt to taste. Serve while hot.

Chapter 3 – Cleaning your Wok

After a full day's work, it won't be unusual seeing your wok demanding clean-up after producing the most delectable dishes. Making stir-fried chicken and your favorite ramen is no joke. In order for your wok to maintain its beauty and for it to be able to serve you longer, you need to properly maintain it. Note that similar to cast iron skillets, wok that is usually made up of carbon steel requires some tender loving care so you need to master the art of cleaning your wok. Here's the good news, it does not really have to be a complicated thing. You only have to remember three things: (1) rinse, (2) scrub, and (3) dry. For you to not get lost or confused, here's a step-by-step guide that you can always go back to for a better cleaning experience.

When your wok has already experienced cooking many stir-fried and other dishes, your steel wok is able to naturally develop a special seasoned coating that makes it nonstick. This special coat even helps improve the flavor of the next dishes you will cook in it. In order to protect this particular coating, you need to avoid the use of anything that is abrasive when you clean your wok. Therefore, a steel wool is a big no-no. Chemically, it is quite unacceptable to use a cleaning agent that is stronger that dish soap.

Truth be told, veteran wok cooks would not even recommend the used of dish washing liquids and related products. More often than not, hot water is more than enough for washing your wok. Together with a cleaning pad, you can assure that your wok is 100 percent clean. For stubborn and sticky food bits, these can be removed by letting the wok hold the water for a while until the food bits are loose enough.

Once your wok is clean, you may now dry your wok. To do this, all you have to do is to place your wok over low heat until all moisture has evaporated. This step should not be missed because if you store a moist wok, rust can develop. You would not want to have a rusty wok.

Conclusion

Thank you again for purchasing this book!

I hope this book was able to help you to cook the best stir-fried meals and other wok recipes.

The next step is to not take our word for it and trying the Wok recipes for yourself. Have fun and enjoy the good food that we have shared with you.

Finally, if you enjoyed this book, please take the time to share your thoughts and post a review on Amazon. We do our best to reach out to readers and provide the best value we can. Your positive review will help us achieve that. It'd be greatly appreciated!

Thank you and good luck!

Check Out My Other Books

Below you'll find some of my other popular books that are popular on Amazon and Kindle as well. Simply click on the links below to check them out. Alternatively, you can visit my author page on Amazon to see other work done by me.

Ultimate Canning & Preserving Food Guide for Beginners

http://amzn.to/1vwrNVP

Cooking for One Cookbook for Beginners

http://amzn.to/THAD6y

Ultimate Barbecue & Grilling for Beginners

http://amzn.to/VNzsVl

The Ultimate Bread Baking Guide for Beginners

http://amzn.to/VCCzzo

Slow Cooking Guide for Beginners

http://amzn.to/1meo2fi

If the links do not work, for whatever reason, you can simply search for these titles on the Amazon website to find them.

Made in the USA
Lexington, KY
28 March 2017